STEM Milestones
Historic Inventions and Discoveries

THE CURIES' RESEARCH WITH RADIATION

Eileen S. Coates

PowerKiDS
press.

New York

Published in 2019 by The Rosen Publishing Group, Inc.
29 East 21st Street, New York, NY 10010

Copyright 2012; revised edition 2019

Editor: Tanya Dellaccio
Book Design: Reann Nye

Photo Credits: Cover Corbis Historical/Getty Images; p. 5 EXPLORER/ Gamma-Rapho/Getty Images; pp. 6, 17 Print Collector/Hulton Archive/ Getty Images; p. 7 https://commons.wikimedia.org/wiki/File:Pierre_Curie_by_ Dujardin_c1906.jpg; pp. 8, 11 Boyer/Roger Viollet/Getty Images; p. 9 Svetlana Pechenkina/Shutterstock.com; p. 12 Time & Life Pictures/ The LIFE Picture Collection/Getty Images; p. 13 https://commons.wikimedia.org/ wiki/File:Becquerel_in_the_lab.jpg; p. 15 (top) Hulton Deutsch/Corbis Historical/ Getty Images; p. 15 (bottom) Universal History Archive/Universal Images Group/ Getty Images; pp. 16,19 (bottom) Hulton Archive/Getty Images; p. 19 (top) UniversalImagesGroup/Universal Images Group/Getty Images; p. 21 Agence France Presse /AFP/Getty Images.

Cataloging-in-Publication Data

Names: Coates, Eileen S.
Title: The Curies' research with radiation / Eileen S. Coates.
Description: New York : PowerKids Press, 2019. | Series: STEM milestones: historic inventions and discoveries | Includes glossary and index.
Identifiers: ISBN 9781538345184 (pbk.) | ISBN 9781538343562 (library bound) | ISBN 9781538345191 (6 pack)
Subjects: LCSH: Curie, Marie, 1867-1934-Juvenile literature. | Curie, Pierre, 1859-1906-Juvenile literature. | Chemists-Poland-Biography-Juvenile literature. | Chemists-France-Biography-Juvenile literature. | Radioactivity-History-Juvenile literature.
Classification: LCC QD22.C8 C577 2019 | DDC 540.92'244 B-dc23

Manufactured in the United States of America

CPSIA Compliance Information: Batch #CWPK19. For Further Information contact Rosen Publishing, New York, New York at 1-800-237-9932

CONTENTS

PARTNERS IN LIFE AND WORK

Radioactivity is when some types of matter give off a form of energy called radiation. Scientists discovered this fact in the late 1800s and have continued to study it ever since. Scientists Pierre and Marie Curie were very successful in studying radioactivity. Their discoveries made them very famous.

Pierre and Marie were married but were also partners in their work. Their discoveries helped other scientists better understand matter and the energy it gives off. The discoveries that stemmed from the Curies' work have helped scientists figure out the different ways that radioactivity can be used to help people and the ways that it can be harmful.

The Curies spent a lot of time in their **laboratory** working on experiments to further their knowledge of radioactivity.

MARIE AND PIERRE CURIE

STUDYING HARD

Pierre Curie was born May 15, 1859, in Paris, France. His father, Eugène, was a doctor. Pierre didn't have a **traditional** education before he went to college. His father and private teachers educated him until he began attending the Sorbonne, a college in Paris, when he was 16.

THE CURIE FAMILY

FASCINATING FINDINGS

When Pierre was 21, he and his brother, Jacques, made a discovery while studying crystals. The brothers found that electricity flows out of certain crystals when they are pressed down on. When the crystals are placed near electricity, they get smaller. They used this information to invent a kind of electrometer, which is a tool that measures electricity.

PIERRE CURIE

Curie graduated from the Sorbonne when he was 18. After graduating, he was a lab assistant at the university. He began studying crystals, which are matter with fixed shapes. A few years later, he began working at the School of **Physics** and Industrial **Chemistry** in Paris. It was there that he began studying magnetism.

A LONG ROAD TO PARIS

Before her marriage to Pierre, Marie Curie's last name was Skłodowska. She was born November 7, 1867, in Warsaw, Poland. She had three sisters and one brother. Her mother, Bronisława, and father, Władysław, were both teachers.

MARIE CURIE

Marie began learning physics and math from her father. She became very interested in the two subjects. She continued to study and learn. However, higher education wasn't available to women in Poland at the time. She took a job teaching and helped fund her sister Bronya's medical education in Paris, France. After Bronya got her **degree**, she paid for Marie to move to Paris and begin her studies in math and physics.

BALANCING FAMILY AND WORK

Marie continued to study in Paris and graduated with her degree in physics in 1893. She was first in her class! She continued studying and graduated second in her mathematics class in 1894. After that, she began working in a **research** lab at the university. She met Pierre through a professor there and quickly began a relationship with him.

The two were married on July 25, 1895. They had two daughters—Irène, who was born in 1897, and Ève, who was born in 1904. Aside from starting a family, the Curies continued researching and working together to make new discoveries.

FASCINATING FINDINGS

The Curies' first daughter, Irène, studied radioactivity, too. Irène and her husband, Frédéric Joliot, discovered a way to **artificially** create radioactive elements. They did this by changing the properties of one element to another. They even won a Nobel Prize—an important award—for their discovery!

Though the Curies spent most of their time doing research, they enjoyed spending time away from their lab, too. After their wedding, they went on a bicycle tour around France.

DOCTORS OF SCIENCE

Both Pierre and Marie continued their studies to earn doctorate degrees in physics. A doctorate degree is the highest level of education a person can get in their field of study. Pierre studied magnetism. He concluded that the temperature of a magnet affects the strength of its pull. This would later be called "Curie's law."

RÖNTGEN AND HIS
X-RAY MACHINE

FASCINATING FINDINGS

Wilhelm Röntgen discovered the X-ray, a kind of ray that can travel through flesh and be used to take pictures of people's bones. Since X-rays go through skin, but not bones, the bones look white in the picture that the rays create.

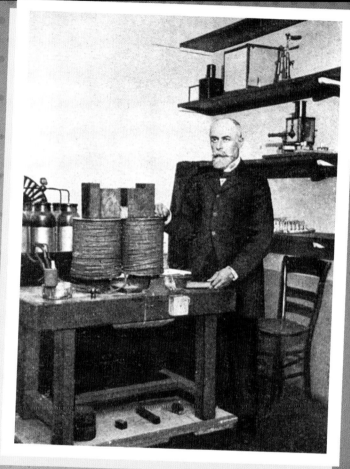

Marie studied what's now known as radioactivity for her doctorate. She learned about the discoveries of two scientists—Wilhelm Röntgen and Henri Becquerel. The two scientists made discoveries about rays of energy and the elements that make them possible. Their work paved the way for the Curies' scientific milestones.

COMING TO CONCLUSIONS

All matter is made up of atoms, which are the smallest possible pieces of an element. Marie figured out that the number of rays uranium gives off doesn't **correspond** with how its atoms are arranged. The only thing that changed the rays' strength was the amount of uranium present, which meant that something inside of the atoms produced the rays.

Marie found that the element thorium gave off rays similar to those of uranium. There were electric currents near the rays, and the more rays there were, the stronger the electric currents were. Using Pierre's electrometer, the Curies separated the matter that gave off the strongest rays, which led them to discover two new elements.

FASCINATING FINDINGS

Atoms are made up of different parts. One of the parts is called a proton. Atoms of an element all have the same number of protons. If the number of an element's protons changes, it becomes a different element.

The couple named one element polonium after the country Marie was born in—Poland. They named the other element radium because of its connections with radioactivity.

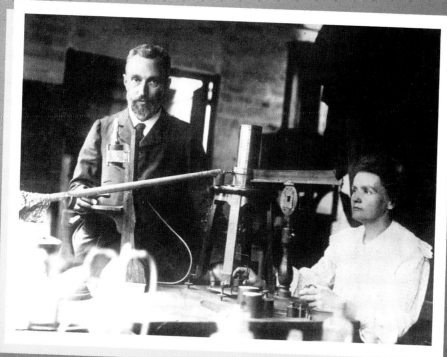

GETTING RECOGNIZED

Together, Pierre, Marie, and Henri Becquerel won a Nobel Prize in Physics in 1903 for their work on radioactivity. Marie was the first woman to receive the award. That same year, Marie also became the first woman in France to get a doctorate degree.

FASCINATING FINDINGS

The Nobel Prizes are awards that are given once a year in six different fields—chemistry, **economics**, literature, peace, physics, and medicine. **Recipients** are chosen based on their **contributions** to each field and are awarded with a medal and a sum of money.

Pierre died in 1906 after being hit by a carriage. Marie chose to carry on with the work they'd done together. She also took over his job as a professor at the Sorbonne. She was the first female professor there. In 1911, Marie became the first person to win two Nobel Prizes. She won the second Nobel Prize for Chemistry for her discovery of new elements.

PUTTING THEIR FINDINGS TO WORK

World War I began in 1914. Marie **organized** X-ray centers to help treat wounded French soldiers. After the war, she worked for the Radium Institute—a new scientific center in Paris. She gave **lectures** on radioactivity around the world and continued researching.

Marie began to study how radioactivity could be used in medicine. Since radiation changes the cells of the body, Pierre thought it might be possible to use it to treat **cancer**. After his death, Marie researched this idea further. She concluded that it could help get rid of cancer. However, people would learn later that too much radiation can have the opposite effect.

Some of the X-ray centers that Marie set up to help treat soldiers were in vans. They were called "petite Curies," or "little Curies."

A LASTING IMPRESSION

Marie Curie died July 4, 1934, from a disease caused by her exposure to radiation. She had health problems caused by radiation for many years before she died.

The Curies' work on radioactivity helped change the world long after their deaths. Pierre and Marie spent their lives to trying to understand radioactivity and the ways in which it can be used. Scientists continue to study the Curies' research to expand on their findings. Today, radiation is the main course of treatment that many doctors use to treat cancer. Many lives have been saved thanks to the Curies.

Marie was exposed to so much radiation during her studies that even the notebooks she used are still radioactive! They have to be stored in a lead box to keep people safe from the radiation they give off.

THE LIVES OF MARIE AND PIERRE CURIE

May 15, 1859
Pierre Curie is born in Paris, France.

November 7, 1867
Marie Skłodowska (later Curie) is born in Warsaw, Poland.

1877
Pierre graduates from the Sorbonne.

1880
Pierre and his brother, Jacques, invent the electrometer.

1893
Marie graduates from the Sorbonne with her degree in physics.

1894
Marie and Pierre meet.

1903
Marie, Pierre, and Henri Becquerel win a Nobel Prize in Physics.

April 19, 1906
Pierre dies in a carriage accident.

1911
Marie wins her second Nobel Prize, this one in chemistry.

July 4, 1934
Marie dies.

GLOSSARY

artificial: Made by people and not by nature.

cancer: A disease caused by the uncontrolled growth of cells in the body.

chemistry: A science that deals with the properties of matter and the changes they go through.

contribution: Something that is contributed, or given.

correspond: To relate to.

degree: An official title given to someone who's completed a course of study at a college or university.

economics: A science concerned with the process or system by which goods and services are produced, bought, or sold.

laboratory: A room or building in which people do scientific experiments and tests.

lecture: A speech given to a group of people about a particular subject.

organize: To put together in an orderly way.

physics: The branch of science that deals with matter and energy, as well as how they interact.

recipient: Someone who receives something.

research: Careful study done to find out new things.

traditional: Following what's been done for a long time.

INDEX

WEBSITES

Due to the changing nature of Internet links, PowerKids Press has developed an online list of websites related to the subject of this book. This site is updated regularly. Please use this link to access the list: www.powerkidslinks.com/hiad/radiation